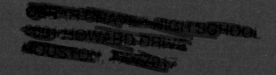

CESAR CHAVEZ HIGH SCHOOL
8501 HOWARD DRIVE
HOUSTON, TX 77017

BADGE *of* VALOR

The NATIONAL LAW ENFORCEMENT OFFICERS MEMORIAL

Brent Ashabranner

Photographs by Jennifer Ashabranner

Twenty-First Century Books
Brookfield, Connecticut

Photograph credits: Courtesy of National Law
Enforcement Officers Memorial Fund: pp. 12
(John M. Gibson), 13 (Jacob J. Chestnut), 19,
31, 35, 38, 41, 42, 43, 44, 45, 46, 47, 49. All other
photographs are by Jennifer Ashabranner.

Published by Twenty-First Century Books
A Division of The Millbrook Press, Inc.
2 Old New Milford Road
Brookfield, Connecticut 06804
www.millbrookpress.com

Library of Congress Cataloging-in-Publication Data
Ashabranner, Brent K., 1921–
Badge of valor: the National Law Enforcement Officers Memorial/by Brent
Ashabranner; photographs by Jennifer Ashabranner.
p. cm.
Includes bibliographical references and index.
Summary: Describes the planning and creation of the National Law Enforcement
Officers Memorial and profiles some of those police officers who gave their lives
in the line of duty.
ISBN 0-7613-1522-5 (lib.binding)
1. National Law Enforcement Officers Memorial (Washington, D.C.)—
Juvenile literature. 2. Police murders—United States—Juvenile literature.
3. Police—United States—History—Juvenile literature. 4. Police—United
States—Biography—Juvenile literature. [1. National Law Enforcement
Officers Memorial (Washington, D.C.) 2. National monuments. 3. Police.]
I. Ashabranner, Jennifer, ill. II. Title.
HV8138.A83 2000
363.2'0973—dc21   00-020222

CONTENTS

This book is dedicated to

JIM BROCK

Twenty-five-year veteran of the
St. Petersburg, Florida, Police Department
and to the memory of his partner

DETECTIVE HERBERT
RAY SULLIVAN

Killed in the line of duty August 19, 1980

ONE

In Valor There Is Hope

The lions drew me in that April morning, as they always do when I visit the National Law Enforcement Officers Memorial. The great bronze jungle cats, two male, two female, watch over the two entrances to the memorial, just as they watch over their cubs, also rendered in dark, burnished bronze. The cubs sleep peacefully with no fear of harm. The adult lions are symbols of the alertness and responsibility that must be a part of the service of all law enforcement officers.

Although it is in a busy part of downtown Washington, D.C., called Judiciary Square, the National Law Enforcement Officers Memorial is a quiet, peaceful place. Its three-and-a-half acres fill the center of the square with islands of grass, trees, and flowering plants. In the spring 14,000 yellow and white daffodils give the memorial an unforgettable radiance. At one entrance to the memorial softly cascading water flows in a beautifully terraced reflecting pool. The marble front of the pool bears this inscription:

THIS MALE LION *is one of two that watch over the northern entrance to the memorial.*

THIS MEMORIAL IS DEDICATED TO
ALL LAW ENFORCEMENT OFFICERS
IN THE UNITED STATES OF AMERICA
INSCRIBED ON THESE WALLS ARE
THE NAMES OF THOSE MEN AND WOMEN
WHO DIED IN THE LINE OF DUTY

The low concave walls of blue-gray marble, one to the east, one to the west, seem to enfold the memorial like comforting arms. On the walls are engraved the names of almost 15,000 fallen law enforcement officers, of whom 154 are women. The names are from every state of the United States and date from the late eighteenth century to the present. Beside each wall is a "pathway of remembrance." The walls and pathways are shaded by double rows of perfectly shaped linden trees.

The spring morning was perfect, and I was one of the few people at the memorial that early. I had wanted the time to myself, to feel once more the specialness of this very special place. I came in at the entrance watched over by the female lions. Some early visitor had already placed a rose in front of one of them, whose pedestal bears these engraved words:

CARVED ON THESE WALLS
IS THE STORY OF AMERICA
OF A CONTINUING QUEST TO PRESERVE
BOTH DEMOCRACY AND DECENCY
AND TO PROTECT A NATIONAL TREASURE
THAT WE CALL THE AMERICAN DREAM
PRESIDENT GEORGE BUSH

President Bush made that statement on the day of the groundbreaking in 1989. Two years later, when the memorial was dedicated, President Bush returned, along with his wife, Barbara, and they placed two roses on one of the walls. Over time a tradition has grown to place roses beside his words. Now it is a rare day when at least one rose will not be seen there.

Something, however, always pulls me to the other female lion on whose pedestal is engraved a single sentence by the Roman historian Tacitus: IN VALOR THERE IS HOPE.

IN VALOR
THERE IS HOPE

A QUOTE FROM BENJAMIN FORGEY *of* The Washington Post *describes this statue: "In all public art there's hardly ever been a gesture more effortlessly affecting than the female forepaw here draped over a wall."*

I have always felt that in those few words lies the very meaning of the National Law Enforcement Officers Memorial. The memorial is not about death. It is about the bravery of men and women who were prepared to die to protect the American dream. It is about valor.

I walked slowly down the eastern wall to look once more at the names on the marble panels. Each wall is made up of sixty-four panels, and a computer has assigned the names on them randomly. Directories at both entrances tell visitors where to find any particular name: what wall, what panel, what line.

I had been to the memorial so many times that my eyes easily picked out names I had located before and that meant something special to me. JAMES LITTLE EAGLE, panel 61E, line 18. James Little Eagle had been a Bureau of Indian Affairs police officer. He was killed in a gun battle on December 15, 1890, when a group of Bureau police attempted to arrest Sitting Bull, the legendary Sioux leader. I have written many books and stories about Native Americans and had once written about that gunfight. Almost all Americans know

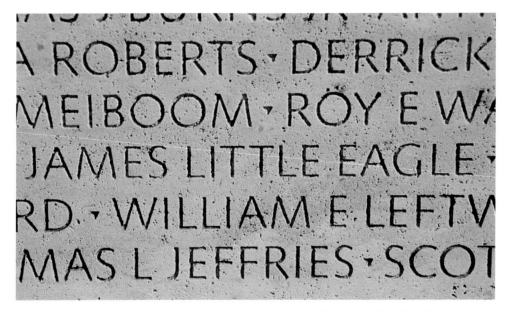

THIS PANEL SHOWS THE NAME *of James Little Eagle, a Bureau of Indian Affairs policeman killed in 1890.*

something about Sitting Bull, but only now are names such as James Little Eagle becoming a part of our nation's memory.

On another panel on the eastern wall I looked once more at the name of Robert Forsyth, a Revolutionary War hero, who was appointed as a U.S. marshal by President George Washington. Forsyth was murdered by pistol fire on January 11, 1794, while serving court papers in a lawsuit. He is one of the first law enforcement officers to have died in the line of duty in the United States. One of his sons later became governor of Georgia, an honor Robert Forsyth did not live to see.

When I reached the lions at the other entrance to the memorial, I stood in front of the one whose pedestal bears these engraved words:

IT IS NOT HOW
THESE OFFICERS DIED
THAT MADE THEM HEROES
IT IS HOW THEY LIVED

They are the words of Vivian Eney Cross, whose husband, Christopher S. Eney, a U.S. Capitol police officer, was killed in a tragic training accident in 1984. His name is on the memorial's western wall.

Each wall of the memorial is 304 feet long, and each of the 128 panels has space for 42 lines, or a total of almost 30,000 names. The blank, unengraved space on both the eastern and western marble walls is a sobering reminder of how many names of future law enforcement officers killed in the line of duty can be inscribed there—almost another 15,000.

I am sure that unhappy thought was on my mind because of the reason that had brought me to the memorial that April morning. April is the month in which new names are added to the memorial walls: the names of law enforcement officers killed in the line of duty during the previous year, plus any newly discovered names from the past. That year the names of 156 officers killed in 1998 would be added and 156 who died in earlier years, including 13 from the nineteenth century, making a total of 312 new names.

ONE OF THE PATHWAYS OF REMEMBRANCE
watched over by the female lions at the south entrance to the memorial

Today a special brief ceremony would be held for two officers whose names were to be added: Jacob J. Chestnut and John M. Gibson. On July 24, 1998, the entire country was shocked by television and radio reports that earlier that day a crazed assassin had charged through the metal detectors at the U.S. Capitol in Washington. He shot U.S. Capitol Police Officer Jacob J. Chestnut in the head even before Chestnut could turn around, killing him instantly. The gunman—later identified as Russell Eugene Weston, Jr., a man with a history of mental illness—then chased a woman down a hallway that led to the office of Texas Congressman Tom DeLay.

Detective John Gibson was on duty at the congressman's office. When he heard gunfire in the Capitol, he told the congressman's staff to take cover, then stepped into the hall. He pushed the woman being chased—one of hundreds of visitors to the Capitol that day—out of harm's way, then exchanged gunfire with Weston. Gibson was struck in the chest; but before he fell he was able to shoot Weston in the thigh and both legs, knocking him down. Weston was quickly taken prisoner by Capitol police. John Gibson was soon carried out, but he died a short time afterward.

Jacob Chestnut was murdered for no reason except that he wore a police officer's uniform, a fate that has befallen hundreds of law enforcement officers. Chestnut was fifty-eight, a Vietnam veteran, a Capitol Police officer for eighteen years. He had been only a few months away from retirement.

By his courageous actions Detective John Gibson undoubtedly saved a number of lives that terrifying afternoon in the U.S. Capitol. After warning the Congressional staff and pushing the woman visitor to safety, he sacrificed his life by standing face-to-face with the killer and dropping him in his tracks.

In a unanimous resolution the House of Representatives authorized the bodies of Jacob Chestnut and John Gibson to lie in state in the Capitol rotunda. Both President Clinton and Vice President Gore attended a memorial service for the officers.

About midmorning several local television crews arrived at the memorial. Shortly after that the widows of Jacob Chestnut and John Gibson arrived, together with members of their families and police and other officials. Capitol Hill Police Chief Gary Abrecht spoke briefly. He said that he hoped the addition of the names of Officer Chestnut and Detective Gibson to the memorial would bring comfort to their loved ones and would ensure that a grateful nation would remember their sacrifice.

"The brightness of this glorious day contrasts with the darkness which remains in our hearts," he said.

Later, with a touch of bitterness, Chief Abrecht reminded reporters that Russell Weston, Jr., the man charged in the Capitol shootings, was still in custody but had been deemed by a judge not mentally competent to stand trial.

Wen-Ling Chestnut, widow of Jacob Chestnut, and Lyn Gibson, widow of John Gibson, did not speak or give statements to the press. They watched silently as their husbands' names were engraved on the memorial's west wall, Chestnut's on panel 39, Gibson's on panel 36. Mrs. Chestnut pho-

JOHN M. GIBSON

A SOLEMN MOMENT.
Lyn Gibson looks at the newly engraved name of her husband, John M. Gibson.

tographed her husband's name being added; Mrs. Gibson placed roses on the pedestal of one of the lions. After taking rubbings of the names, the widows and their loved ones left the memorial. Soon the television crews left, as well as the others who had attended the name-engraving ceremony.

I stayed on a bit longer. It was noon now, and two or three people came from nearby buildings to eat their bag lunches. Others walked through the memorial on their way to lunch or meetings. A man and woman with a young girl arrived and looked for a name on the western wall after consulting the

WEN-LING CHESTNUT *photographing the engraved name of her husband, Jacob J. Chestnut, on the memorial's west wall*

name directory. They, too, had brought a basket lunch and ate it in the shade of the arbor in the center of the memorial.

The memorial really is a place of life, I thought, and it fits perfectly in this busy part of our nation's capital. I remembered something Craig Floyd, chairman of the National Law Enforcement Officers Memorial Fund, had once said: "It was meant to be a memorial park, not a cemetery."

As I left, I paused for a moment to watch some birds happily taking baths in the reflecting pool.

JACOB J. CHESTNUT

TWO

The Need for a Law Enforcement Officers Memorial

A merica's great national memorials have come from the deep-seated belief of many Americans that a certain person, group, or period in our national life deserved a special place in the history and memory of our country. Sometimes the effort to create a memorial has taken a long time. The Washington Monument was not completed until more than a hundred years after it was started. Congress authorized a Lincoln Monument Association in 1867, two years after Lincoln was assassinated, but the Lincoln Memorial was not finished until fifty years after the great president's death.

In a few cases the time has been short. The Women in Military Service for America Memorial was built within fifteen years of the time the American Veterans Committee began a campaign for it in 1982. Congress authorized a Vietnam Veterans Memorial in 1980. Astonishingly, the memorial was built and dedicated just two years later. Both the Vietnam Veterans Memorial and the Women in Military Service for

14

America Memorial were built with the contributions of private citizens, groups, and businesses. No government money was used.

In most cases, one person, with a few strong helpers, has been the moving force behind the creation of America's great memorials. Without the long and tireless efforts of Senator Shelby Cullom of Illinois the Lincoln Memorial might never have been built. Jan Scruggs, himself a wounded Vietnam veteran, dreamed of a Vietnam Veterans Memorial, believed in it and fought for it when many people laughed at the idea of such a memorial. Brigadier General Wilma L. Vaught saw the Women in Military Service for America Memorial as "a gift to the American people," and she worked day and night for more than ten years to make that gift a reality. Sculptor Korczak Ziolkowski envisioned the monumental Crazy Horse Memorial on a mountain in South Dakota and worked at it for almost thirty-five years with his own hands.

The need for a national memorial honoring officers killed in the line of duty had been felt for a long time by law enforcement organizations, several influential politicians, and a determined group of law enforcement leaders. The need was most strongly felt by the wives, husbands, and other family members of slain law officers.

Clearly needed was greater public awareness of the dangers of law enforcement and the readiness of law officers to face mortal danger when necessary. The law enforcement profession knew those dangers well enough. Every year 38 million crimes are committed in America—an average of more than one crime *every second*. On the average, more than 63,000 law enforcement officers are assaulted each year; of that number 21,000 are injured, many seriously. There was no complete information on the number of law enforcement officers who had lost their lives doing their job. The Federal Bureau of Investigation did not begin to keep statistics on line-of-duty deaths in all branches of law enforcement until 1961. One thing was certain: The figure was in the thousands. The deadliest known year in law enforcement was 1974, when 271 officers were killed. The deadliest decade was the 1970s, when a total of 2,204 officers died in the line of duty.

A national law enforcement officers memorial would honor those who had sacrificed their lives to protect Americans from crime. And those who believed in such a memorial were sure it would also accomplish other important purposes, such as reminding Americans of the courage and dedication to duty required of law officers. Throughout its history the nation had seemed to take those qualities for granted, and there indeed had been a tendency, perhaps stemming from America's frontier days, to give crime and outlawry a romantic cast.

Such criminals and cold-blooded killers as William H. Bonney (Billy the Kid), Butch Cassidy and the Sundance Kid, Bonnie and Clyde, John Dillinger, Pretty Boy Floyd, and Baby Face Nelson had in fact attained a kind of status as folk heroes. Scores of books have been written about them, and

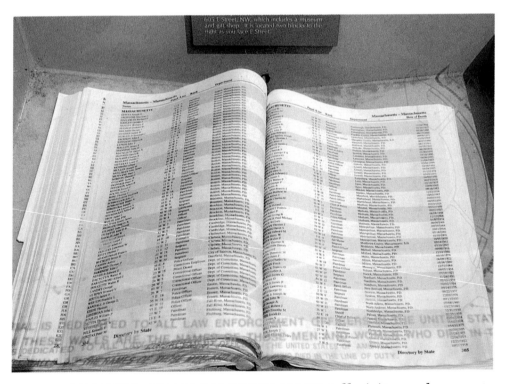

DIRECTORIES AT EACH ENTRANCE *tell visitors where to find names on the memorial walls.*

myriad movies and television programs made about them. Some of these felons were even beginning to appear in video games! Without a memorial, who would remember the eleven officers killed by the Bonnie and Clyde gang? The sheriff, the four Indiana officers, the trooper, and the federal agents killed by the Dillinger gang? The six lawmen slaughtered by William Bonney?

Perhaps as important as anything else, a memorial could help change the negative view of law enforcement officers held by many Americans. This negative feeling had long been nourished by newspaper and television spotlights on reported cases of police corruption, excessive force, and false arrests. While such problems and failings of course should be made public, there was little reporting of the faithful, courageous, and skillful service of the overwhelming percentage of law enforcement officers.

Without doubt, public esteem of law enforcement reached a low point in the socially discontented decade of the 1970s. In those years thousands of young men and women marched in the streets of American cities shouting, "Death to the pigs." The "pigs" were the officers of all branches of law enforcement, sworn to protect the rights and safety of all lawful citizens—even those who were marching in the streets verbally abusing them.

The certainty that a National Law Enforcement Officers Memorial was badly needed took deeper root during the violence and negative atmosphere of the 1970s. Before a national memorial or monument of any kind can be built on United States government land, however, it must be authorized by an act of Congress, and the bill must be signed into law by the president. The bill must be introduced in the House of Representatives by a congressman and in the senate by a senator. The hard work of shepherding the bill through Congress falls on them.

Those who believed in a National Law Enforcement Officers Memorial were certain that they knew the right congressman to sponsor a bill for a memorial in the House of Representatives. His name was Mario Biaggi, congressman from the 19th

A STUDENT GROUP *from Traverse City, Michigan, brings a wreath to the memorial to place beside the newly added name of Dennis Warren Finch, a member of the Traverse City Police Department who was killed in 1998. When the memorial was created, it was hoped that it would be a positive force on the public and would help remove the negative image of law enforcement held by many in the 1970s.*

District of New York City, a district in which he represented people from the boroughs of the Bronx and Queens and also the city of Yonkers. The story of Mario Biaggi is an American success story to its very core. He was born in Harlem in 1917 to poor Italian immigrants. His father, Salvatore, earned a living as a marble setter. His mother, Mary, worked as a cleaning woman. By the age of twelve, even while going to school, Mario was helping his mother clean buildings and was also delivering bags of laundry for five cents a bundle. By the time he graduated from high school, he was making eight dollars a week as a foreman in a factory on New York's West 28th Street.

Looking for a step up, Mario Biaggi became a substitute letter carrier for the U.S. Postal Service and later a regular carrier. After working for the postal service for nearly six years, he decided that he wanted to become a New York City police officer. In 1942, after scoring at the very top in the police entrance examination, Biaggi became one of "New York City's Finest." He was then twenty-five years old. He began as

MARIO BIAGGI WAS INSTRUMENTAL *in the development of the memorial. He served as a New York City police officer for twenty-three years.*

a cop on a beat, and in a career that spanned twenty-three years, he worked his way up to the rank of detective lieutenant. While on the police force, Biaggi was wounded ten times in the line of duty. He received twenty-eight heroism commendations, making him the most decorated police officer in New York City history when he retired. One of his many awards was the Medal of Honor for Valor.

At the age of forty-five and near the end of his career as a police officer, Biaggi decided that he wanted to become a lawyer. There was one major problem. He did not have an undergraduate college degree, a requirement for entering law school. Because of his distinguished career as a police officer, the American Bar Association—in a very rare move—decided to let Biaggi enter law school without a college degree. He received a full scholarship from the New York Law School and began to attend classes at night while still on the police force. When he retired from the New York City Police Department in 1965, he studied law day and night and completed the three-year program in two-and-a-half years. He was admitted to the New York Bar in 1966 and began to practice law. He specialized in public interest cases such as helping mentally retarded persons receive better care in state institutions.

After two years as a lawyer Mario Biaggi made another major career decision. He ran for a seat in the United States Congress and won. In all succeeding elections he won by overwhelming margins, as high as 94 percent of the popular vote. His legislative efforts in child-abuse prevention, crime prevention, and benefits for the elderly and handicapped were outstanding.

In 1972 a delegation of Suffolk County, New York, law enforcement officials proposed to Congressman Biaggi that he introduce a bill that would authorize the building of a National Law Enforcement Officers Memorial. No one in Congress could have understood better than Mario Biaggi the need for such a memorial. After discussions Biaggi agreed to draft the necessary legislation. He was joined by U.S. Representative James R. Grover, Jr.

The timing could not have been worse. The last of the American military forces, together with all American Embassy personnel, just had been driven from Vietnam. America's disenchantment with the Vietnam War was deep and intense. The country was in no mood to think about honoring heroes. There was little Congressional support for a law enforcement officers memorial, and the idea went nowhere.

Seven years later the national atmosphere was different. A small group of Vietnam War veterans, led by Jan Scruggs, had rallied the country to build a Vietnam Veterans Memorial that would honor not the war but rather the 58,000 young Americans who had died in the war. The memorial was dedicated in November 1982.

It was in that same year that a common cause brought the national law enforcement community together as never before: a determination to push for legislation that would ban the production of armor-piercing "cop killer" bullets that can penetrate bulletproof vests worn by police. Many law enforcement groups from all over the country came to Washington to lobby Congress to vote for the ban. Outlawing armor-piercing bullets was high on Congressman Biaggi's legislative list.

The hope for a National Law Enforcement Officers Memorial had never disappeared. With the Vietnam Veterans Memorial to encourage them and the effort to ban armor-piercing bullets to unite them, a group of law enforcement officers again visited Biaggi. They asked him once more to sponsor a bill to authorize the building of a memorial honoring law officers killed in the line of duty.

Biaggi was still as much in favor of such a memorial as he had ever been. He agreed to draft the necessary legislation for the House of Representatives but only on the condition that law enforcement officers and their organizations throughout the country would work hard to support it. The answer was an enthusiastic yes. Law enforcement communities everywhere began to let Congress know the importance of a memorial to them.

THE VISITORS CENTER *is located two blocks from the memorial. More than thirty exhibits cover the history of the memorial and law enforcement in America.*

Mario Biaggi had now been a member of Congress for almost fifteen years. He had become known as a skillful politician with an outstanding legislative record. He moved the law enforcement memorial resolution through the House smoothly, gathering many cosponsors. With the encouragement of law enforcement organizations in his state, Claiborne Pell, the senior senator from Rhode Island, introduced a resolution for the memorial in the Senate. Senator Pell's reputation as a respected elder statesman ensured that the memorial resolution would move smoothly through the Senate.

Believing that Congress would authorize the memorial, Biaggi, Pell, and Suzanne Sawyer, head of an organization called Concerns of Police Survivors (COPS), formed a nonprofit foundation called the National Law Enforcement Officers Memorial Fund and incorporated it in the District of Columbia. The board of directors was made up of fifteen selected national law enforcement organizations. Craig Floyd, a member of Congressman Biaggi's legislative staff, was appointed executive director and later became chairman of the fund. The purpose of the new organization was to raise the money necessary to build the memorial and to decide what it should look like and where it should be placed.

On October 1, 1984, the resolution to build the memorial was passed by the House of Representatives. Four days later it was passed by the Senate. Two weeks later, on October 19, the resolution was signed as Public Law 98-534 by President Ronald Reagan. The new law did the following:

- Authorized the National Law Enforcement Officers Memorial Fund to build a memorial honoring law enforcement officers who die in the line of duty. The memorial was to be built on federal land in the District of Columbia or environs.

- Gave the Secretary of the Interior, together with the Commission of Fine Arts and the National Capital Planning Commission, authority to approve the memorial's design and location.

- Specified that construction of the memorial was not to begin until the Secretary of the Interior was sure that enough money was available to complete the memorial.

- Specified that no government money was to be used in the memorial's construction.

- Stated that construction of the memorial must begin within five years of the bill's signing or authority to build the memorial would expire.

Law enforcement officers throughout the country relished their sweet victory. Only after the excitement died down did the questions begin. How do you design a national memorial? How do you find the right location? Where do you find the millions of dollars necessary to build it?

No one had the answers to those questions, but five years seemed like enough time to find them.

THREE

Creating the Memorial

T ime melts quickly in the world of busy people, and everyone connected with the National Law Enforcement Officers Memorial Fund was very busy. The memorial's board of directors met, exchanged ideas, and kept in touch by letters and phone. Some effort was made to raise funds through volunteer activity at local levels. But by 1986, after two years, no work had begun on a design for the memorial; no search for a location for the memorial had started; and only $47,000 in funds had been raised. Based on the cost of the Vietnam Veterans Memorial, an estimated $8 million or more would be needed for the National Law Enforcement Officers Memorial—$47,000 was little more than one-half of one percent of that amount!

As executive director of the National Law Enforcement Officers Memorial Fund, Craig Floyd shouldered the main burden of organizing and energizing the effort to build the memorial. Floyd, however, was a senior member of Mario

Biaggi's staff and had his hands full with the congressman's ambitious legislative agenda. But the five years to start building the memorial had now shrunk to just three years, and almost nothing tangible had been done. Floyd knew one change that would happen immediately: Working sixteen-hour days would become a part of his routine.

Craig Floyd's career on Capitol Hill had begun as a congressional intern. He joined Mario Biaggi's staff in 1978, when he was hired to be a legislative correspondent. He had been a lifelong resident of the Washington, D.C., area and had graduated from the local George Washington University with a degree in journalism. He might not know how to build a memorial, but he did know Washington, D.C., and how things got done in that very special city.

What Craig Floyd did was pick up the phone and call someone who did know how to build a memorial—he called Jan Scruggs. The Vietnam Veterans Memorial, behind which Scruggs had been the driving force, had become the most visited memorial in Washington, D.C. Floyd did not know Jan Scruggs, had never even met him, but he had a hunch Scruggs was a nice guy, and Floyd's hunch was right. When he told Scruggs who he was and why he needed advice, Scruggs said sure, they could talk, and they arranged a meeting.

That meeting became a major takeoff point for the National Law Enforcement Officers Memorial. Jan Scruggs listened to Floyd and sensed behind the law enforcement memorial the same motivation that had inspired the creation of the Vietnam Veterans Memorial: the desire to honor men and women who died in the line of duty, heroes who had not received the recognition from America that they deserved.

At that time Jan Scruggs's great work of building the Vietnam Veterans Memorial was behind him, and he was then president of the Vietnam Veterans Memorial Fund; but he had decided that he wanted to become a lawyer and planned to enter the University of Maryland Law School. Scruggs's interest in the National Law Enforcement Officers Memorial was so strong that he offered to help until his law classes began a few months later.

Craig Floyd was delighted to have Scruggs's vast experience to draw on, and Scruggs's input was immediate and substantial. Scruggs introduced Floyd to two of his friends, George W. (Sandy) Mayo, a Washington lawyer, and Robert Frank, who had his own accounting firm in northern Virginia. Both men had helped Scruggs with the Vietnam Veterans Memorial. The result of their meeting with Floyd was that Mayo became legal counsel for the National Law Enforcement Officers Memorial Fund, volunteering his services, and that Frank became the fund's treasurer and accountant. They have continued their work for the fund ever since.

Floyd talked to Jan Scruggs about getting started on a design for the law enforcement memorial. Scruggs reviewed the history of the Vietnam Veterans Memorial design. A national design competition had been held that drew 1,421 entries. The winner was the powerful black wall design by Maya Lin, at that time an architectural student at Yale University.

The national competition had been a great success, but, as Scruggs pointed out, it also had been time-consuming and expensive—neither of which luxuries the National Law Enforcement Officers Memorial Fund had. Scruggs suggested it would be better for the fund to find and commission an architect to design the memorial.

Floyd and his colleagues did just that, discussing their conception of the memorial with a number of architects and looking at their work. Their final choice was Davis Buckley, a Washington architect who had designed many outstanding buildings and who clearly was deeply challenged by the idea of designing a national memorial to honor fallen law enforcement officers.

The final design of the memorial would have to wait until a site was found, but Buckley listened to ideas from the law enforcement community and attended memorial services for officers killed in the line of duty. In his mind there began to grow the picture of a memorial that would be a place of quiet beauty, of trees and grass, where people could walk and reflect, where the family of a fallen loved one could feel they were in a place of peace.

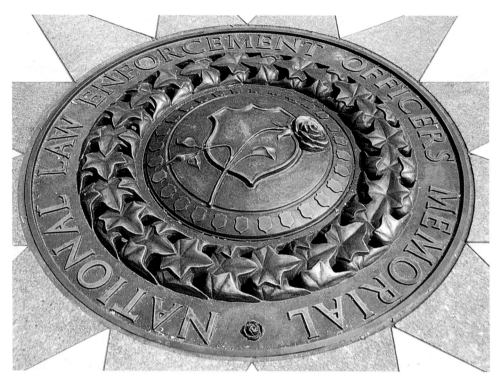

THE LOGO OF THE *National Law Enforcement Officers Memorial is a blue shield with a red rose across it. The shield is the universally recognized symbol of law enforcement. The blue color represents the "thin blue line" of law enforcement officers. The red rose is a symbol of remembrance and respect for the officers who have given their lives in the line of duty. This large bronze medallion is located in the pavement design at the very center of the memorial.*

From the beginning all National Law Enforcement Officers Memorial Fund business had been conducted in Mario Biaggi's congressional office. Jan Scruggs convinced Craig Floyd that the fund should have its own separate office and that a press conference should be held to kick off a major fund-raising campaign. Floyd called on one of his friends, Pat Rowland, who got the fund rent-free office space.

In December 1986, Biaggi and other memorial supporters held a press conference at the National Press Club to get the message out all over the country that building the National

Law Enforcement Officers Memorial was very much on track. They appealed for financial help from corporations, businesses, private organizations, and especially individual citizens who believed that such a memorial had a meaningful place in America.

An old hand at fund-raising, Jan Scruggs turned his attention to attracting corporate sponsors and had early success with a $20,000 donation from the Borg-Warner Corporation and $25,000 from Pepsi-Cola. Other businesses followed suit; personal checks from private citizens began to arrive, some for as little as $1, others for $5, $10, sometimes $20 or more. Police and other civic-minded organizations began to contribute. Millions would be needed to build the memorial, but a good start had been made.

Craig Floyd knew that a strong and truly dedicated board of directors for the National Law Enforcement Officers Memorial Fund was essential. During this time he spent long hours building such a board. When he had finished, the fund board of directors consisted of representatives of fifteen prominent law enforcement organizations:

- Concerns of Police Survivors
- Federal Law Enforcement Officers Association
- Fraternal Order of Police
- Fraternal Order of Police Auxiliary
- International Association of Chiefs of Police
- International Brotherhood of Police Officers
- International Union of Police Associations/AFL-CIO
- National Association of Police Organizations
- National Black Police Association
- National Organization of Black Law Enforcement Executives
- National Sheriffs Association

- National Troopers Coalition
- Police Executive Research Forum
- Police Foundation
- United Federation of Police

While there are hundreds of smaller local law enforcement groups throughout the country, these national organizations represented virtually every person in law enforcement in America. Craig Floyd was sure the memorial fund now had the kind of strength and support it would need for the future. The search for a place to build the National Law Enforcement Officers Memorial began in January 1987.

Washington, D.C., is a city of monuments and memorials. Some, such as the Lincoln Memorial, are awe-inspiring. Some are dramatic: the sky-piercing Washington Monument and the U.S. Marine Corps Memorial of the flag-raising on Iwo Jima. The Vietnam Veterans Memorial black wall of names is heart-breaking. A walk through the memorial to President Franklin D. Roosevelt is a walk through American history. All of these memorials and many others are located in or near the great memorial corridor that begins at the United States Capitol and continues on an axis through the National Mall and ends across the Potomac River at Robert E. Lee's home, Arlington House, in Arlington National Cemetery. Almost without exception, the supporters of new memorials hope that their memorial can be located in the great memorial corridor. The problem is that very few empty sites remain in the corridor.

The site search for all new memorials approved by Congress is led by the National Park Service. After a site is found, it must be approved by the National Capital Memorial Commission, the Commission of Fine Arts, and the National Capital Planning Commission.

The National Park Service assumed that the National Law Enforcement Officers Memorial Fund would want its memorial in the memorial corridor if that was possible. The Park Service had in mind a place along Memorial Drive, the broad roadway just across the Potomac leading up to Arlington National Cemetery. There were already several memorials in front of the hedgerows that line both sides of the drive. Among them were a lovely small memorial to the Seabees, the Naval Construction Battalions; a memorial to a great fighting unit, the 101st Airborne Division; and a statue called *The Hiker*, commemorating the Spanish-American War.

There were still a few spaces for memorial statues or monuments along Memorial Drive. The Park Service recommended that the law enforcement officers memorial be put in one of them. But that was not what the National Law Enforcement Officers Memorial Fund had in mind at all. They wanted a setting large enough for people to gather for ceremonies and celebrations. They wanted more than just enough space for a single statue. Also, a location that close to Arlington National Cemetery would inevitably link the law enforcement mission with the military mission. That did not seem like a good idea.

The fund officers responded with a suggestion that the law enforcement officers memorial be built on the Ellipse, the grassy area between the White House and the Washington Monument. Nothing was there, and it would provide just the kind of space they had in mind. The National Capital Memorial Commission was shocked at this suggestion. The Ellipse was some of the most precious land in Washington, the commission said. Because of its location, nothing could ever be built on it that could be identified with only one special group or cause. The commission denied the request.

So the search for a site went on for months, with discouraging results. Some sites were too remote, some too small, some in unattractive parts of the city or environs. Sometimes, however, when the outlook is bleakest, someone comes up with an idea that works. In this case that someone was John Parsons of the National Park Service.

One day Parsons called Craig Floyd and asked, "What about Judiciary Square?"

Judiciary Square? Floyd knew where Judiciary Square was, but what he knew about it was not exciting, to say the least. Judiciary Square is in a busy part of downtown Washington, surrounded by office buildings; it is not close to the monumental corridor or other famous Washington tourist attractions such as the Museum of Natural History or the Air and Space Museum. It was, in fact, a run-down public plaza with a few scruffy park benches and two off-center Metro subway elevator towers. It had been described by a Washington newspaper as a disgrace to the city, and that description would have been hard to dispute.

But, as John Parsons pointed out, Judiciary Square was federal government land and therefore a place where a memorial might be put. The square was large enough for the kind of memorial envisioned by the National Law Enforcement Officers Memorial Fund. And the fact that Judiciary Square was a stop on Washington's underground Metro system was a great plus because visitors could easily reach a memorial built there.

For all those reasons the Judiciary Square site did make good sense to Floyd and the other fund officers. As he investi-

A VIEW OF JUDICIARY SQUARE *before it became the site of the National Law Enforcement Officers Memorial*

gated the site and researched its history, Floyd became convinced that Judiciary Square was much more than a good location for the National Law Enforcement Officers Memorial. It was the *perfect* place. The judicial system and law enforcement in America are inseparably bound together. And in this section of Washington—as the name Judiciary Square implied—many national and local courts were located, as were the headquarters of the Federal Bureau of Investigation and Metropolitan Police headquarters. The part of Judiciary Square the memorial would occupy was surrounded on three sides by buildings of the Superior Court of the District of Columbia. Nearby were the U.S. District Court, the United States Court of Appeals for the Armed Services, and other courts, including one building with the sign POLICE COURT on it.

As Floyd's research would reveal, two centuries of history hung over Judiciary Square. In 1789, President George Washington had commissioned Pierre Charles L'Enfant, the gifted French architect who had fought for the American colonies during the Revolutionary War, to draw up plans for a new Federal City, which would become the capital of the new United States of America. The name *Washington* would be given to the city, although the president had not requested that honor.

In his plans, submitted in 1791, L'Enfant had envisioned a national capitol building that would be the seat of the legislative branch of government, a presidential mansion (the White House) that would be the center of the executive branch of government, and an area of the city (which became Judiciary Square) that would be the judicial center of government.

Given this history, there seemed no doubt that a law enforcement officers memorial should be located there. The National Capital Memorial Commission gave its approval to the location in March 1989, and the other review agencies agreed. The National Law Enforcement Officers Memorial now had a home.

But the selection had taken more than two years, and to meet the law's deadline, construction of the memorial had to begin in seven months! The agencies that oversee and approve memorials and other public construction in Washington—the National Capital Memorial Commission, the Commission of Fine Arts, the National Capital Planning Commission, the National Park Service—were intensely interested in what the National Law Enforcement Officers Memorial would look like. Craig Floyd remembers that he and architect Davis Buckley attended more than fifty meetings with those committees to discuss plans and details of the memorial.

In the end, however, as finally approved, the memorial did not fundamentally differ from Buckley's original concept. In

ARCHITECT DAVIS BUCKLEY *faced a special problem with two Metro towers in the center of the memorial site. The towers could not be removed, so he incorporated them into the memorial design. He surrounded them with striking metal pergolas (arbors with a latticed cover supported by posts) and enclosed them with tall, leafy honey locust trees.*

his vision of a memorial park, he had the strong support of over 30,000 interested Americans who had sent their ideas to the memorial fund. Over 94 percent of them wanted the memorial to be in a peaceful setting with trees, grass, and flowers.

The people most concerned with building the memorial had assumed almost from the beginning that a statue of a law officer or group of officers would be a central part of the memorial. But finally they found it impossible to decide what kind of statue it should be. There was no way to represent in a single statue or even a small group of statues all branches of law enforcement and all kinds of law enforcement officers. Should the statue be uniformed or plainclothed? Police or sheriff? State trooper or federal marshal? Male or female? Black, Hispanic, or white?

A brilliant answer to the problem was finally found by Davis Buckley and Washington sculptor Raymond Kaskey. There would be statues, but they would be symbolic of the protection provided by law enforcement officers rather than a portrayal of the officers themselves. They would be lions.

As Kaskey explained, "Throughout history, from the Gates of Nineveh to the present, lions have been used to represent not only power, but also courage, protection, alertness. All of these things we wanted to put across with the symbolic representation in the memorial."

Benjamin Forgey, *The Washington Post*'s highly respected writer about the city's architecture and memorials, had this to say about the lions: "Superbly conceived, splendidly executed, subtly differentiated, and perfectly placed, they won review board hearts, and they'll win yours."

The walls of names of officers who died in the line of duty are the heart of the National Law Enforcement Officers Memorial. Yet the decision to have the names came late and only after long debate. The memorial fund's board felt for a long time that finding all of the names of fallen officers throughout the nation's history would be an overwhelming job.

But in September 1988 the board agreed that regardless of financial and research problems, the names must be a part of

SCULPTOR RAYMOND KASKEY *working on the clay model of a male lion that would be cast in bronze for the memorial*

the memorial. The board's first thought was to engrave on the walls only names of officers who had been killed since 1961, when the FBI began to keep fatality figures. Soon, however, the unfairness of that policy became apparent. It would bring disappointment to thousands of wives, children, and other relatives of officers killed in the line of duty before 1961. They would visit the memorial and look in vain for the name of a loved one.

The final decision was to engrave on the walls all names of officers killed in the line of duty, reaching as far back into the nation's history as possible. A recommendation by John Parsons of the National Park Service to list the names randomly removed the problem of trying to list them alphabetically or by date of death (a problem that has been a continuing one for the Vietnam Veterans Memorial).

ALL NAMES ON THE MEMORIAL WALLS *have been engraved by Jim Lee (left) and Kirk Bockman of Great Panes Glassworks, Denver, Colorado. To date they have engraved almost 15,000 names. The process is time-consuming work. A rubber stencil with the names on it is made first and taped on the walls. The engraving is done with a compressed air machine that blasts into the marble to a particular depth. After engraving, the depth of each name must be measured to ensure that all names will wear evenly over the years.*

The criteria to be eligible for listing on the memorial walls were carefully spelled out. Most important, the officer had to have been killed while doing his or her duty as an employee of a local, county, state, or federal law enforcement agency. The officer had to have been duly sworn to duty with full arrest powers. Exceptions to those conditions could be made but only with careful review.

The memorial fund's small staff went to work diligently, contacting more than 15,000 law enforcement departments throughout the country for information about line-of-duty deaths. They also examined years of newspaper microfilm for reports of law enforcement officer fatalities. A great deal of information came from private citizens writing in about the death of a family member. All such leads were carefully verified. By dedication day, 12,561 names had been engraved on the memorial walls. New names would be added every year, and the search for names would never end.

After twenty years of distinguished service, Mario Biaggi left Congress in 1988. Craig Floyd could now devote all of his time and energy to the National Law Enforcement Officers Memorial, and—although he had many other attractive career possibilities—he made the decision to do so.

On Monday, October 30, 1989, ground was broken for the National Law Enforcement Officers Memorial. The ground-breaking ceremony in Judiciary Square was attended by President George Bush, Attorney General Dick Thornburgh, FBI Director William Sessions, and many other dignitaries that included U.S. senators and representatives. All members of the fund's board of directors were present, as well as two thousand other law enforcement officers and survivors of fallen officers from all over the country.

The ceremony began at two o'clock, and President Bush gave the keynote address. He spoke movingly of the many sacrifices that law enforcement officers make, ". . . the thin blue line that protects our nation from the evil within." And the president mentioned ". . . the brave spouses and parents and children who pay a terrible price in loneliness and loss when a law enforcement officer dies in the line of duty."

When Craig Floyd spoke, he said, "There will be tears on this site today—tears for a lost friend or loved one. But those tears can now be followed by warm smiles because, after more than two hundred years of service and sacrifice, American law enforcement officers will finally receive the national tribute they have deserved for so long."

And, in what was clearly a mixture of pride, thanks, and humility, Floyd said, "It wasn't easy to get here . . . but we've made it. . . ."

After the speeches ended, the high point of the ceremony came: Shovels bit into the ground, the earth of Judiciary Square was turned, and the building of the National Law Enforcement Officers Memorial began.

On October 15, 1991, the completed memorial was dedicated. In the two years following the groundbreaking ceremony, architect Davis Buckley and his project manager, Tom Striegel, had worked magic in shabby Judiciary Square. Sculptor Raymond Kaskey and his assistant, George Carr,

GROUNDBREAKING—OCTOBER 30, 1989! *A great day in the history of the memorial. Shown (left to right) are Craig Floyd, President George Bush, Chicago Police Chief Greg Jaglowski, and Attorney General Dick Thornburgh.*

had created the magnificent guardian lions and their trusting cubs. Craig Floyd and his happy but exhausted board of directors and staff had taken care of literally thousands of details, great and small, necessary to building the memorial. They had also raised the $11 million needed to cover its cost. The money had come from 300 corporate sponsors and a heartwarming one million private citizens.

President Bush declared October 15, 1991, to be National Law Enforcement Officers Memorial Dedication Day, a public day of commemoration and celebration for all Americans. Two days of special events preceded the dedication ceremony. One of them was a march from the U.S. Capitol to the memorial at Judiciary Square by ten thousand law officers, survivors of line-of-duty tragedies, and supporters. A solemn event that lasted twenty-four hours was the "Roll Call of Fallen Officers." The names of all 12,561 law enforcement officers on the new memorial's walls were read aloud by 160 readers from every state in the Union.

At the dedication ceremony speaker after speaker expressed appreciation for the beautiful new National Law Enforcement Officers Memorial and gave their thanks to those who had made it a reality. Perhaps no one spoke with more feeling than Barbara Dodge, at that time national president of Concerns of Police Survivors, when she said: "You have given fallen law enforcement men and women a place of honor in our nation's capital. You have given the families and friends of these officers a promise—a promise etched in stone—that the sacrifices of our loved ones will never be forgotten."

FOUR

In the Line of Duty

The statistics of crime in America are grim, sometimes frightening. For example: the FBI reports that in 1996 alone more than four thousand assaults against officers occurred when they responded to domestic disturbance calls. Since records have been kept, more than five hundred officers have been killed responding to such disturbances. More than nine hundred local, state, and federal law enforcement officers have been killed when struck by vehicles while they were directing traffic or when outside their car investigating road problems. More than one hundred police officers have been killed in bank robberies through the years.

Behind impersonal figures such as these are the names of real men and women who were officers of the law. Their names—14,993 of them after the newly added names of 2000—are now engraved on the blue-gray marble walls of the National Law Enforcement Officers Memorial. Behind every name is the story of a human life that ended before it should have. Here, briefly told, are a few of their stories from the memorial fund's deep files.

SHERMAN C. GRIFFITHS
BOSTON POLICE
DEPARTMENT
Panel 15 East, Line 9

They called him the Gentle Giant. Detective Sherman Griffiths worked in the Boston Police Department Drug Control Unit. He did not like to throw his weight around, but he was always the first man through the door at a drug bust. "He was the best door man in the drug unit," said one of his police colleagues. "He knew he could make a difference. That's what he was doing when he gave his life."

On the night of February 18, 1988, Detective Griffiths was where he always was, standing outside the door of an apartment, ready to be the first man through on a drug raid. Hardly had the first sledgehammer slammed into the heavily reinforced door than a hail of gunfire erupted from inside the apartment. All of the police raiding squad except Griffiths was able to hit the floor and crawl to safety. But Griffiths, standing in front, was struck in the head and fell back. He died a few hours later without regaining consciousness.

Sherman Griffiths left behind a wife and two young daughters. He also had six brothers, one of whom had joined the Boston police force. Six years later, in March 1994, three more of his brothers finished their cadet training and were sworn in to the Boston Police Department. A year later still another brother joined the force.

Veterans of the Boston Police Department all agreed that the Gentle Giant would have been very, very proud.

LINDA CAROL HUFF
IDAHO STATE POLICE
Panel 14 East, Line 21

There was no sane reason for what happened that June night in 1998.

Trooper Linda Huff of the Idaho State Police had stopped at police district headquarters to complete some reports. When she left the office and crossed the parking lot to return to her patrol car, gunshots rang out from the darkness. The ambusher fired seventeen rounds from a 9-millimeter handgun. Trooper Huff was struck ten times, but even as she lay on the pavement, mortally wounded, she drew her pistol and returned the gunfire. She died at the scene; but she hit her assailant in the neck and body, wounding him badly. He was captured quickly and later convicted of first-degree murder.

The death of Linda Huff illustrates one of the many dangers that law enforcement officers face—motiveless murder. There have always been criminals and mentally unstable people who carry out an impulse to kill a law enforcement officer just because of the uniform he or she is wearing. These deadly attacks are hard to guard against because they are senseless and come with no warning.

Linda Huff left behind two sons, ages ten and four, and a five-year-old daughter. Her husband was also an Idaho state trooper. They had been sworn in together in a ceremony at the Idaho state capital. Before becoming a trooper, Linda Huff had been a sergeant in the Payette County sheriff's office for five years.

"She always faced forward," said Payette County Sheriff Bob Barowsky, "with a smile on her face and a love for life."

SAMUEL P. COWLEY
FEDERAL BUREAU OF
INVESTIGATION
Panel 30 West, Line 16

The Great Depression of the 1930s was a time of notorious gangsters, many of them carrying out their crimes in the American Midwest. This was also the era of the "G-Men," the Federal Bureau of Investigation agents whose top priority was to find the gangsters and stop them.

Heading up the drive to get rid of gangsters was FBI Agent Samuel P. Cowley. Cowley had become known as a fearless and brilliant crimefighter, and he was sent from Washington headquarters to find the gangsters and bring them in or kill them if need be. Cowley and his FBI team moved swiftly. Together with local police in Ohio, they found and killed Pretty Boy Floyd when he resisted arrest. That same year John Dillinger, who was responsible for the death of eight law enforcement officers, was hunted down and killed in a gun battle with FBI agents.

Finally, on November 27, 1934, Cowley and Special Agent Herman Hollis located Baby Face Nelson in a car near Barrington, Illinois. In a running gun battle Hollis was killed, and Cowley was mortally wounded. But Cowley kept firing, and finally Baby Face Nelson went down. He died soon of his bullet wounds.

Fearless to the end, Sam Cowley had done his job.

SAUL MARTINEZ
HIGHWAY PATROL,
CALIFORNIA
Panel 48 East, Line 20

It was after midnight when California Highway Patrol Officer Saul Martinez and his partner James Rice saw the abandoned car. What was it doing parked on the shoulder of a lonely desert highway? Why was it facing the wrong way? They stopped to investigate, but as they walked toward the car, Martinez saw the blinding headlights of another car. It had veered off the road at high speed and was hurtling straight at the Highway Patrol officers.

"I heard the sound of crunching gravel, and I heard Saul yell *run*," James Rice said afterward. "But everything went into slow motion for me, and Saul pushed me—slammed me— out of the way."

In those nightmarish two seconds Saul Martinez saved his partner's life instead of jumping to safety himself. The careening car struck Martinez with full force, threw him down the highway, and landed on top of him. Help soon arrived, but Martinez died without regaining consciousness. It was later determined that the man driving the car was under the influence of alcohol and prescription drugs.

Afterward, California Governor Pete Wilson called Highway Patrolman Saul Martinez "a hero who earned life's crown" for sacrificing his life to save his partner's. "It was courage above and beyond what few, if any, of us can muster," the governor said.

The National Law Enforcement Officers Memorial is a tribute to the nearly 15,000 officers who have given their lives in the line of duty. At the same time it is a tribute to the 750,000 law enforcement officers at the local, state, and federal levels who every day devote themselves to making the United States a safer place to live.

The National Law Enforcement Officers Memorial Fund has a program that focuses on the outstanding work being done by law enforcement officers in every part of the country today. The program is called Officer of the Month, and it features the officer selected on the memorial fund's web site calendar and in press releases. Lee Caudle, who is in charge of selection and who worked with Craig Floyd on his radio program "America Under Siege," explains the selection criteria:

"The foremost requirement is that the officers have exceptional law enforcement credentials, with proven accomplishments. We didn't necessarily want cops who were making the headlines. We wanted people who are making a difference. We wanted officers who were recommended by their fellow officers or the citizens they serve."

And Lee adds, "We weren't looking for heroes, just dedicated police officers who were doing their jobs with honor, dignity, and devotion."

Here are a few of the Officer of the Month selections.

BARRY G. WASHINGTON
TEXAS DEPARTMENT OF
PUBLIC SAFETY
Officer of the Month—
November 1997

When his patrol car was passed by a black truck racing down the highway at great speed, Trooper Barry Washington had a strong hunch that the driver of that truck wanted to be chased. Washington was thoroughly familiar with drug smugglers' diversionary tactics, so he radioed to troopers ahead about the speeding truck and resisted the impulse to go after the speeder himself. In only a few minutes another truck came down the highway, an innocent-looking rental truck driven by a woman. Washington pulled the woman over and discovered that she was hauling a not-so-innocent load of over half a ton of marijuana.

It is the seasoned experience of over fifteen years, laced with incidents such as this one, that has made Barry Washington one of the top law enforcement officers of the Texas Department of Public Safety. Besides taking part in countless manhunts and investigations of robberies and other crimes, Washington has an astonishing 490 drug seizures to his credit. Throughout his career as a trooper, he has received twenty-one citations for outstanding police work.

Barry Washington joined the Texas Department of Public Safety in 1982 after graduating from the Texas Law Enforcement Academy. Before that he had earned a college degree in education and taught school for two years. Despite his demanding schedule as a trooper, Washington has kept his interest in teaching alive by volunteering some of his off-duty time as a tutor of high school students. He works especially with those students who have athletic ability but who cannot participate in school sports because of low grades. From time to time he has also taken parentless children into his family and assumed the responsibility for raising them.

Trooper Barry Washington's concern for helping others is clearly as big as the state he lives in.

JEFFREY MULLER
U.S. PARK POLICE OFFICER
WASHINGTON, D.C.
Officer of the Month—May 1997

It was a bitterly cold night in January 1997. U.S. Park Police Officer Jeffrey Muller was on patrol duty in Washington, D.C., near the Anacostia River when he came upon a car stalled in the middle of the road. An elderly man standing beside the car told Muller his car had run out of gas. He identified himself as Claude Carter and a woman inside the car as his wife, Mary.

Muller returned to his patrol car and was preparing to radio for help when he saw with shock that the stalled car had begun to roll backward toward the river—with Mrs. Carter still inside. Muller rushed to the moving car and tried to get the door open, but it was too late. The car broke through a retaining wall and plunged into the river, the trunk completely submerged, the front bumper hooked precariously on a piece of the wall.

Muller raced back to his car, called for emergency help, and returned to the river. He jumped in without hesitation but could not get the car door open. He scrambled out of the river and ran to his car for a life-saving ring and rope; but just as he returned, the car in the water broke loose from the wall and drifted away from shore.

Again with no hesitation, Muller plunged into the icy water and swam to the sinking car. Still unable to open the door, he smashed the window with his service revolver and pulled Mrs. Carter out. Now almost overcome with hypothermia, Muller managed to swim to shore with the nearly unconscious woman. Officers responding immediately to the emergency signal pulled Mrs. Carter and Muller from the water, and within seconds they were both safely on their way to the hospital.

For his heroic efforts that cold January night, Jeffrey Muller received the Park Police Medal of Honor, a rare award that has been given only twice before in Park Service history.

SABRINA M. CURRAN
DEPUTY SHERIFF
HARNETT COUNTY, NORTH CAROLINA
Officer of the Month—October 1997

Something wasn't right, and Detective Sabrina Currin felt it with a sixth sense that comes only with years of experience. She had been called to a hospital to investigate the death of a baby in which child abuse was suspected. Currin began to question the baby's father. So sharply directed were her questions that after a few minutes the man jumped up and bolted down the hall in a frantic bid to escape. Detective Currin chased him down, brought him down, and arrested him on the spot.

In her fourteen years as a deputy sheriff (with the rank of detective) in the Harnett County Sheriff's Office, Sabrina Currin has built a solid record of accomplishments in child abuse and sex abuse cases. One of her former supervisors calls her "the best I've ever seen" in such cases. And her current supervisor, Captain Jerry Lamm, says, "When others go home, she stays until she gets the job done. She's very intelligent, a very thorough investigator."

Currin played a major role in the establishment in Harnett county of a rape crisis center, one of her most important accomplishments. North Carolina Secretary of State Elaine Marshall, who worked with Detective Currin in establishing the rape crisis center, gave her high praise. "She really identifies with the victims," Marshall said. "Her dedication is unsurpassed."

Like any good law enforcement officer, Sabrina Currin does the job that the moment of crisis requires. She and a fellow officer were once on their way to lunch when a radio bulletin alerted all officers to be on the lookout for two suspected cop killers. When the suspects' car was spotted, Currin and her colleague were in the vicinity. They immediately joined the chase and helped make the capture. Lunch had to wait that day.

Outside her official duties as a law enforcement officer, Sabrina Currin is fully involved in community affairs. She is director of the local chapter of Mothers Against Drunk Driving. At Christmas time she helps her father collect food and other holiday items for donation to needy families in the county.

STEPHEN NASTA
NEW YORK CITY POLICE
DEPARTMENT
Officer of the Month—
September 1996

Inspector Stephen Nasta was the first law enforcement officer chosen to be Officer of the Month by the National Law Enforcement Officers Memorial Fund. His story is a classic one of ability, dedication, and hard work receiving its just reward.

Steve Nasta was seventeen when he decided he wanted to be a New York City police officer. He took the New York City Police Department's entrance examination and scored in the top 100 of an estimated 20,000 applicants. Nasta began as a trainee in 1964 when he was eighteen and continued in that status for three years, since the minimum age to become a New York City police officer is twenty-one.

Crime in New York City rose an alarming 91 percent between 1965 and 1971. The principal reasons were increasing inner-city poverty, growing drug abuse, and youth unrest. Serious riots occurred in 1964 and 1968. Steve Nasta began his service with the New York City Police Department during those years, assigned first as a policeman in the 106th precinct. He was in that assignment until 1973 and in that time received seven departmental medals for outstanding police work. One citation was for disarming a shotgun-wielding man on a crowded subway platform. Another was for preventing a distraught man from committing suicide by jumping from the ledge of a tall building. Nasta tried for several minutes without success to persuade the man to come back inside the building. When the man started to jump, Nasta lunged at him and pulled him to safety. It was a highly risky action that almost cost Nasta his life, but to him it was just doing what his job called for at that moment.

In 1973, at the age of twenty-seven, Nasta was promoted to sergeant and assigned as patrol supervisor for the 67th and 101st precincts. It was also in 1973 that he began night classes at City University of New York's John Jay College of Criminal Justice. He continued his night study for years until he earned both a bachelor's and a master's degree in criminal justice.

In the years that followed, Nasta rose steadily in rank from sergeant to lieutenant to captain to deputy inspector and finally, in 1996, to inspector. In all those years perhaps no assignment was harder than when, as lieutenant in 1981, he implemented an antinarcotics program called Operation Pressure Point in the Lower East Side of Manhattan, at that time a place of rampant crime and overrun by heroin dealers. In the first week of the program Lieutenant Nasta's command made 1,700 arrests. Operation Pressure Point was a four-year, seven-days-a-week, twenty-four-hours-a-day undertaking that steadily reduced crime in the area.

As he rose in rank, Nasta continued to be assigned to antinarcotics work. When he was appointed inspector, he was commanding officer of more than four hundred narcotics investigators and undercover officers in the Bronx.

Stephen Nasta retired from the New York City Police Department in 1998. Upon retirement he had the satisfaction of knowing that he had been a part of one of the greatest turnarounds in police history. Felony crimes in New York City were at their lowest levels in twenty years. Relations between New York City's citizens and the police had improved greatly, and Nasta's Community Policing Team in the Bronx had played an important part in the improvement.

What does a retired inspector do after thirty-five years of police work in New York City? Move to Finger Lakes country and go fishing every day? Take up easy living in Florida? Not if he happens to be Stephen Nasta. The former inspector is beginning his retirement by going to work for the Bronx district attorney's office. His new job? Chief detective investigator.

And if that is not enough to keep him occupied in his retirement, Steve Nasta is teaching courses as an adjunct professor at the John Jay College of Criminal Justice.

FIVE

The Candlelight Vigil

By congressional law passed in 1962, the president is authorized to proclaim May 15 of every year as Peace Officers Memorial Day and the calendar week in which May 15 falls as National Police Week. A later law specifies that flags should be flown at half-staff on May 15 to honor the thousands of law enforcement officers who have died in the line of duty. Many ceremonies and observances of Peace Officers Memorial Day are held by police organizations throughout the country.

In Washington, D.C., a candlelight vigil always held on May 13, two days before Peace Officers Memorial Day, has become a tradition that brings thousands of law enforcement officers, their families, and the survivors of fallen officers to the nation's capital. The vigil is held at the National Law Enforcement Officers Memorial and is the centerpiece of the memorial fund's Police Week activities. Other activities include a law ride (motorcycle procession), a National Police

Survivors Seminar, law enforcement training seminars, a pipe band procession, and other programs.

The candlelight vigil brings all of the law enforcement visitors together in one place on one night. By program time for the 1999 vigil the crowd would swell to more than 15,000, the largest gathering in the vigil's eleven-year history. Perhaps it was the thought that this would be the last candlelight vigil of the century that had brought so many. Perhaps they just wanted to be there.

Jennifer and I arrived more than an hour before sunset, but already several thousand people were there. At the memorial entrances everyone was given a small white candle and candle guard, the candle to be lit later in the program. Busloads of women and children arrived, survivors of police tragedies who were attending seminars at a nearby hotel. Each one carried a long-stemmed red rose. They were saluted by a police honor guard flanking the walk by the reflecting pool.

THE HONOR GUARD *at the candlelight vigil. The vigil is held at the National Law Enforcement Officers Memorial each year on May 13.*

The walls of the memorial were now lined from end to end with photographs, flowers, wreaths, handwritten messages, uniform insignia, and other mementos in recognition of names on the walls. Some of the bottom names, I noticed, were darker than the ones above them, a sad reminder that they had been added in just the last few weeks. Soon the engraving stain would be faded out by weather and rain, and the new names would blend with the others.

DURING NATIONAL POLICE WEEK *in May the walls of the memorial are filled with flowers, wreaths, photographs, handwritten messages, uniform insignia, and other mementos.*

The program began at dusk, and the master of ceremonies was Craig Floyd, just as he had been from the first candle-light vigil eleven years before. On the platform with him were Janet Reno, longtime attorney general in President Bill Clinton's cabinet; Mario Biaggi; Debbie Geary, National President of Concerns of Police Survivors; and John Walsh, producer of the television show *America's Most Wanted: America Fights Back*. On this night Mr. Walsh would receive the National Law Enforcement Officers Memorial Fund's 1999 Distinguished Service Award. When Floyd presented the award later in the program, he noted that *America's Most Wanted* had been directly responsible for assisting law enforcement with the capture of 563 felony criminals.

"We have all heard the news," Craig Floyd said in his introductory speech on this vigil night. "Crime is down. The nation's murder rate has fallen to its lowest level in thirty years. America is a safer place to be." And Floyd concluded, "On the walls that embrace us here tonight are the names of nearly fifteen thousand law enforcement officers who have made the ultimate sacrifice in the performance of duty. They are a constant reminder of just how much our law enforcement professionals are willing to give to keep America safe."

In her position as attorney general Janet Reno is the highest-ranking law enforcement officer in the nation. When she addressed the crowd, she forcefully called for greater gun control and emphasized that 40 percent of the officers whose names had just been added to the memorial walls—those killed in 1998—had been killed by guns. On a personal note Ms. Reno said that she sometimes walks in the memorial alone, to look at the names and to contemplate.

Debbie Geary's husband, David, an officer in the Metro-Dade, Florida, Police Department, died in the line of duty on November 28, 1988. Debbie was pregnant with their second child at the time of her husband's death. She later organized the South Florida chapter of Concerns of Police Survivors and in 1998 became national president. Tonight she spoke to the thousands in the audience—the wives, the children, the moth-

ATTORNEY GENERAL JANET RENO *was the principal speaker at the candlelight vigil held in 1999. In her speech she mentioned that she has attended every candlelight ceremony at the memorial in her six years as attorney general.*

ers, fathers, sisters, brothers, the husbands—with the name of a loved one engraved on the memorial.

"We cannot take away the pain you are feeling, but we can be there with you through your pain. We would like to replace the cold feeling with a feeling of warmth. . . . After all the candles are lit and the memorial is illuminated only by candle glow, think how many candles it took to produce that light. Think how many people are here tonight that care about you. Allow them, allow us, to lighten your burden."

At the end of the program Janet Reno and Debbie Geary each lit a candle. Members of the Concerns of Police Survivors National Board then came to the dais to light their candles from those. The board members left the dais and lit candles held by some of the vigil attendees. They in turn lit the can-

MANY YOUNG PEOPLE ATTEND *the candlelight vigil to remember and honor friends and loved ones who served in law enforcement and gave their lives in the line of duty.*

dles of people sitting or standing near them, who went on to do the same with their neighbors. Soon the National Law Enforcement Officers Memorial was suffused with soft candlelight. Some people embraced; some stood silently in small groups. The beautiful words of "Amazing Grace," sung by the Police Department Choir of Durham, North Carolina, filled the memorial.

When the vigil ended, the names of the 312 officers that were added to the memorial in 1999 were read from the dais. Janet Reno began the reading, and others from the states of the slain officers took part. After the reading of the names, people began to leave the memorial. Some walked to the Metro station, others to the buses that would take them back to their hotels.

But a number of people remained at the memorial even after the name-reading was over. Some stood talking quietly. Some walked slowly along the paths, viewing the walls now lined with flowers, wreaths, photographs of fallen officers, and handwritten letters addressed to names engraved on the walls.

As we left, Jennifer said to me, "These people are remembering."

And I said, "That's what memorials are for."

Information About

THE NATIONAL LAW ENFORCEMENT OFFICERS MEMORIAL

THE MEMORIAL IS LOCATED on E Street between 4th and 5th streets in northwest Washington, D.C.

THE MEMORIAL IS OPEN twenty-four hours a day every day of the year.

VISITORS CAN REACH THE MEMORIAL easily by Metro subway. There is a Metro stop at Judiciary Square where the memorial is located.

VISITORS CENTER: The National Law Enforcement Officers Memorial Visitors Center is located at 605 E Street, NW, less than two blocks from the memorial. The center has many exhibits that tell the history of the memorial and of law enforcement in America. The center has a gift shop featuring items relating to law enforcement. The Visitors Center is open 9:00 A.M. to 5:00 P.M. Monday through Friday, 10:00 A.M. to 5:00 P.M. Saturday, noon to 5:00 P.M. Sunday.

FOR MORE INFORMATION or to arrange group tours, write or call the Visitors Center.

Mailing address:	National Law Enforcement Officers Memorial 605 E Street, NW Washington, D.C. 20004
Telephone:	(202) 737-3400
Fax:	(202) 737-3405

A GREAT DEAL OF INFORMATION about law enforcement in the United States of America can be obtained from the National Law Enforcement Officers Memorial Fund Web Site: **www.nleomf.com**

BIBLIOGRAPHY

Ashabranner, Brent. *Their Names to Live: What the Vietnam Veterans Memorial Means to America*. Brookfield, CT: Twenty-First Century Books, 1998.

Clark, Connie. *The Making of a Memorial*. Washington, D.C.: The National Law Enforcement Officers Memorial Fund, 1992.

Fernandez, Maria Elena. "For Capitol Police, Nothing Is the Same." *The Washington Post*, November 23, 1998.

Forgey, Benjamin. "Lions of Valor: The Officers' Memorial." *The Washington Post*, October 12, 1991.

Greene, Marcia Slacum. "For Slain Police, Two Walls of Honor." *The Washington Post*, October 16, 1991.

Greenwalk, Rachel. "Families, Colleagues of Slain Police Officers Find Solace at Memorial." *Morning Star-Telegram* (Fort Worth, TX), May 31, 1993.

Italia, Robert. *Courageous Crimefighters*. Minneapolis: Oliver Press, 1995.

Schomp, Virginia. *If You Were a Police Officer*. New York: Marshall Cavendish (Benchmark Books), 1998.

Wheeler, Linda. "A Memorial Uses Life to Honor Dead." *The Washington Post*, April 6, 1995.

———. "Work Begins on Memorial to Police." *The Washington Post*, October 21, 1989.

Wirths, Claudine. *Choosing a Career in Law Enforcement*. New York: Rosen Publishing Group, 1997.

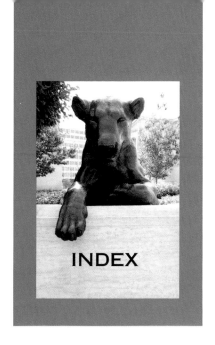

INDEX